1

Rough Country Trading Post

P. O. Box 127

Dinosaur, Colorado 81610.

Wagner, John A

The Magnificent Wild Mustangs

Of Sand Wash Basin, - 2nd ed.

Printed in the U.S. A.

2nd ed. March 13, 2015

Book design by John Wagner

Photographs by John Wagner

The Magnificent Wild Mustangs

Of Sand Wash Basin

John A Wagner

This book is dedicated to all Wild Mustangs.

May they always run free!

Very few people have a gift for capturing the true beauty of nature in photographs. John Wagner is one of those rare people. He has used his love and knowledge of the often rocky, gorged, and sandstone red and tans of northwest Colorado and eastern Utah enhanced with his outdoor skills to create poetry through the eyes of a photographer. I believe you will agree when you have seen and admired the magnificent photographs in this book. Marvel at the beauty, appreciate the difficult simplicity and recognize the talent and time it took to create such pictures.

There were several albums of John's photographs on the coffee table full of nature photographs, various scenery and animals, especially horses, and a magnificent series on an eagle. The photographs were as good as or better than any of the numerous nature photographs I see incorporated in calendars, posters, postcards, and the like. The pictures were especially impressive knowing that John was not some highly trained photographer who had studied in college or art school. In fact John was neither. He is self- taught with his own photography technique. His camera was a moderately priced digital Canon SLR which he uses without a tripod.

John told of us his plans to make a book from the eagle pictures. He had followed it from egg to flight, and the pictures were magnificent, rich, and colorful. It was a view of nature seldom captured in such detail. John and his wife have discussed other projects, perhaps a children's book. Whatever further they decide to do it is clear that John is a true and skilled outdoorsman who has endured often dangerous terrain, wild animals and climates to explore his passion for photography that captures the beauty and essence of his natural theater. Yes, John is my first cousin and I, myself, am just a small cheaper digital camera shooter, point and click, I do appreciate great photography. The passage of 48 years would seem to dilute any perceived bias.

My wife agreed that these were great photographs as did many others that have viewed some of them since; family, friends and acquaintances. Now is your turn, reader and viewer, I think you will agree that these beautiful pictures are the treasures of a nature lover and a true artist that should be shared.

And yes, he still collects a rock now and then! He told us he had picked up one just that day and added to the collected pile in his yard.

Ron Wagner- Las Vegas, Nevada

Sand Wash Basin Mustangs

Wild Horses are an American Heritage and You (The Public) should fight for their freedom by writing your BLM, contacting your senators, congressmen, governor, and the President of The United States. Please help save Our Wild Horses.

My personal belief: "Let them run proud and free."

This photo album will show you the way of life of bands (herds) of Wild Horses located in an area called Sand Wash Basin. Sand Wash lies about 17 miles to the northwest of Maybell, Colorado, on Highway 318.

Sand Wash Basin is a huge area, it covers over 160,000 acres of public lands between Seven Mile Ridge and the Vermillion Bluffs. Just think that is roughly 250 square miles of rolling hills, small bluffs, steep ridges, washes and gullies. During a heavy down pour the dry washes and gullies become fast moving streams. The low spots holds lots of much needed water, also the waterholes on the high benches provide water to the Wild Horses and other wildlife.

This area is used by OHV, rock hunters, photographers, hikers, and other activities.

This is the Home for the Wild Horses. There are over 400 animals in this vast area. The colors of these horses vary from grays to blue roans, chestnuts to paints, buckskins, bays, palominos. Some have unique markings and patterns, like Picasso, Hoot, and Cowboy.

The grasses don't look like much, but they are highly nutritious, and the Wild Horses are very healthy, as you will see in the pages of this book. Sand Wash is also the home to hawks, eagles, deer, antelope, rabbits, sage grouse, burrowing owls, prairie dogs, chipmunks, coyotes, bobcats, mountain lions, rattlesnakes, and many other critters.

It was almost midnight before I could get to sleep. I was going to Sand Wash Basin to see the Wild Mustangs. I haven't been there in years and just the thought of going back into some of my old stomping grounds made me happier than a bear eating honey.

Sand Wash Basin was roughly 70 miles from my home in Dinosaur, Colorado, and it wouldn't take long to get there. My cameras were cleaned, batteries were charged; spare batteries, extra SD cards and Compact Flash cards, were in the camera bag. I also had water, food and other items to survive, if I needed to.

Sleep came slowly and my dreams were vivid with Wild Mustangs, and of all things, a huge hungry T-Rex. The T-Rex was chasing the Mustangs, and I was trying to lead him away from the young foals, when I tripped and did one humdinger of a belly flop in the sand. Horses were squealing, the T-Rex was almost upon me, just then the alarm went off, and I about killed the pillow in my bed before I got awake.

When I came out of the bedroom my hair was sticking straight up, which I don't have much of. I must have looked a sight, because my dog, Buddy, barked at me and growled.

"Buddy." I said. "It's me I promise."

He looks closer at me and begins to wag his tail. What do you expect I would look like after wrestling a T-Rex pillow to death?

After getting my bearings back, I gathered my gear and stacked it in one corner of the living room floor.

My wife comes into the room and takes one look at the pile, and said, "Are you leaving for one day or a year?"

"But Baby Doll, it's only a few things and I might need them."

"Do you have everything?" She asked with a shrug of her shoulders.

"Let's see, cameras, cards, batteries, soft cleaning rags, canteen, water, compass, notebook, pencils, pens, food, chapstick, bug dope, binoculars, knives, flint and steel, pistol and shells, hiking staff, and two backpacks of miscellaneous gear. Did I forget anything?"

"Where's the Ice Chest?" she asked.

About an hour later, my in-laws, Joe and Wanda, pulled into my driveway. It didn't take me to long to load my gear. Even though my wife thought I should have rented the Mayflower to haul all my gear.

Ha-ha! I got it all stuffed into Joe's van. Nothing to worry about, except, the trunk lid wouldn't shut. Shoot! I had to leave a few items. My wife gave me that "I told you so" look.

Then we were off like a stampede of Wild Mustangs. I was so excited that I almost asked Joe if we were there yet. But I contained myself and kept my yap shut.

Finally, we reached the turnoff to Sand Wash Basin. I told Joe that the hills had changed a lot; there were 4-Wheeler and Dirt Bike tracks everywhere. Just before we reached the BLM Holding Corral, I pointed out a ridge, and told Joe and Wanda that ridge use to have Tipi rings on it. I wondered if they were still there or if they had been destroyed?

Monument Hill looked the same. The old trail going by it went up to the base of the Juniper covered ridge. The barren grayish formation at the base of the ridge use to have a lot of petrified wood scattered on it. I wondered if there was any left on it.

After crossing a small wash, we headed up a small dug-way. The slopes of the dug-way held brown and black chert and pieces of petrified algae. As we continued on up, my eyes were scanning the ridges and valley for horses. As we topped out, I spotted the first Band of Wild Mustangs to the east about a thousand yards away. We stopped and looked at them with are binoculars and then continued on down County Road 67 past the first waterhole, then on past County Road 48. Just before we got to the second waterhole, Joe and I both saw the Wild Horses at the same time. There were over thirty of them, and more down at the waterhole. The van doors flew open before Joe came to stop, and with our cameras in hand, it was Clicking Time.

My clicking finger was really getting an exercise. No rigor-mortis now. The horses didn't pay much attention to us and we were getting some excellent shots. There were three different herds; one band down by the waterhole had a handsome palomino stallion (Corona), a band to the northeast about 300 yards had a magnificent white stallion (Cosmo), and another band to the north about 250 yards had an awesome pinto stallion (Picasso). It was totally awesome!

So readers turn the page and start viewing these Magnificent Wild Mustangs of Sand Wash Basin.

This Paint is called Picasso. He is an amazing stallion, with all those patterns of colors. He is also one of the most famous stallions of the Sand Wash Basin. Everyone that knows about Picasso looks for him, and his picture has been taken thousands of times. Picasso is very tolerant of people. Most of the times you can get close enough for very sharp pictures. Even if you just own a point and shoot camera, you should still get good pictures that you will treasure forever.

Picasso is over 20 years old and he has survived many long, hard winters. Picasso knows how to take care of his band.

So if you find him, have respect for this awesome stallion, and click that camera.

Happy Shooting!

This colt is named Falcon because of a mark on his neck that resembles a falcon. The mare behind him with the piece of bunchgrass in her mouth is Falcon's mom, her name is Lark, and both of them belong to Eagle's Band.

At the time I took this picture, Eagle had 4 in his band; there was Lark, Falcon, Hoot and Sparrow.

If you noticed they were named after birds, and the names fit them to a tee.

Falcon is one of my favorite colts. What do you think? Is Falcon your favorite too?

Here is Falcon again. Can you find the mark that gives him that name?

The day I took this picture I was about 25 yards away from Falcon and I got 100's of pictures of him. The wind was howling and I was sitting down, and Eagle, Lark, Falcon and Hoot were feeding close to me.

Eagle the stallion of the band, knew I was no threat, so I became part of his herd for over an hour.

It was a day I will always treasure and I hope you will treasure the Wild Mustangs of Sand Wash Basin too.

This Stallion is called Hoot. He is Falcon's older brother. I love this Mustang, he is one awesome horse. The wind was whipping his mane, but he didn't have to worry about wind knots, his mane was too short.

Hoot came within 300 feet of me and began to graze. To him I was just another member of the band and since I wasn't eating any of the grass, I was okay by him.

Corona

This Magnificent Stallion's name is Corona. He is a Band Stallion and another favorite for the Watchers of Sand Wash Basin. Corona is very tolerant of people and you can get pretty close to this hunk of Stallion. I always look for Corona because I know I can get at least 300 feet from him and his band.

Corona is known as a Dunalino, because of the dark dorsal stripe down his back, and stripes on the inside of his legs.

Silverado

Flirt

Davy Greasewood

Cabellero

Picasso

This is called the snaking posture. Where a stallion puts his head down low to inform his band that they need to go in the direction he wants.

All stallions do the snaking posture. I love watching them, especially when one horse in the band wants to go a different way. The stallion seems to get really agitated. But he will keep on the tail of that horse until it goes the way he wants.

Picasso is always chasing his mares. I think the mares do it on purpose just to drive him crazy.

What do you think?

Cowgirl

Eagle's Band, Lark, Falcon and Hoot.

PJ

This young colt is named after his sire Picasso. PJ stands for Picasso Junior.

When he was first born Picasso hid his band, and I took a lot of road trips to Sand Wash Basin searching for him. When I was about ready to give up, there he was.

I fell in love with this little colt. Joe and Wanda Tosh said his tail looked like a foxtail. If you've ever seen a red fox, I'm sure you will have to agree.

Wanda said. "Let's call him PJ."

Joe and I agreed. From then on PJ was his name.

Cowboy

Splashing away

Ellie and Flirt

Mango

Picasso and His Band

Picasso, Mango, and Mingo

PJ

PJ

PJ

PJ

Corona and Band at the waterhole

Hoot

Lark, Falcon and Hoot

PJ and his mom Olga

Cosmo and Band at the waterhole

Don't take my picture, said Cosmo.

Willie Nelson

Zeus is one handsome stallion

Cosmo and Band at the waterhole

Bear is one tough stallion

Picasso and his son Snip

Blue is a red roan, and he is totally awesome.

Picasso

Picasso and Snip

Picasso and Snip

Sage (Femur)

Corona

Cimarron

Cheyenne

Corona

Viggo's Band

Tulip

The amazing Tulip

Little Heidi

Rounder

Ranger

Ranger

Miss Destiny

Apache

Miss Destiny and her mom, Kira.

Tag

Centauro

Voodoo

The Palominos

The Fight

Cosmo at the waterhole

The Prince of Sand Wash Basin

Centauro

Centauro

Cosmo snaking

Cowboy and Voodoo

Nick

Prince

Hawk

Craig and Outlaw

Olga and her son PJ

PJ, Olga and Picasso

PJ

PJ

Jimmy Dark Sand

Prancer prancing

Aragon and Zeus

Heading for the waterhole

At the Waterhole

Who are you?

Prince's Band

Come on, Hoot. Let's play.

I'm a Wild Horse from Sand Wash Basin

Eagle

Voodoo and Cowboy

Eagle on the run

Picasso on the run

Miss Maddy the little pink horse

Em

Cosmo and Band

Eagle of Sand Wash Basin

Stirring up mud

Kiowa and Nick

Bug in the ear.

Picasso and Band

Mango

Mingo and Mango

Jet the Force of Sand Wash Basin

The Wild Mustangs

The Force of Sand Wash Basin

Making dust

Snow Man

Viggo's Band

White Out and Band

White Out and Band

Half Moon

Prince of Mud

Mango

Falcon

Yellow Cat and Blazer

Splashing is fun

Still Splashing

Now that you've reached the end of the book, I hope you have enjoyed their incredible Journey through my pictures. Now reader, you can help these Horses by contacting your local BLM office about how you can help keep the Wild Mustangs free.

Thank You,

John Wagner

Note to readers:

I feel that all animals should be respected and I have always done so by not disturbing their habitat or them. Any time the mustangs appeared upset by my presence, I would back away and wait for another opportunity.

I strongly encourage everyone to show all of God's creature's kindness and respect.

I live in Dinosaur, Colorado with my wife Sarah, my daughter Megan and our dog Buddy.

I have been blessed to have had this experience with one of God's awesome creations the wild horse.

Look for more of my works as God provides them.

www.ingramcontent.com/pod-product-compliance
Lightning Source LLC
Chambersburg PA
CBHW041500280526
45792CB00004B/1081